ULTIMATE
FIDGET
SPINNER
GUIDE

Text and illustrations copyright © 2017 by Penguin Random House LLC
All rights reserved. Published in the United States by Random House Children's
Books, a division of Penguin Random House LLC, New York. Originally published in
paperback as *Ultimate Fidget Spinner* by Penguin Random House UK,
London, in 2017.

Random House and the colophon are registered trademarks of
Penguin Random House LLC.

Visit us on the Web! rhcbooks.com

Educators and librarians, for a variety of teaching tools, visit us at
RHTeachersLibrarians.com

Library of Congress Cataloging-in-Publication Data is available upon request.

ISBN 978-0-525-57934-2 (trade paperback)

Printed in the United States of America

10 9 8 7 6 5 4 3 2 1

First Edition

ULTIMATE
FIDGET SPINNER
GUIDE

JONATHAN COOK

RANDOM HOUSE 🏠 NEW YORK

Contents

WHAT IS A FIDGET SPINNER?

Fidget Spinners are small toys, usually made out of plastic or metal, that spin around a ball bearing. Some people claim that playing with them helps you to **pay better attention in class** or **concentrate** on what you're doing, or that they are good for making you **feel less anxious.** Kids with ADHD (Attention Deficit Hyperactivity Disorder) or autism may find them really useful for this.

How do they work?
It's all in the spin. The activity of making the toy spin around can be really relaxing and help you to feel calmer!

Have you got ants in your pants? Fidgeting is when you just can't sit still! You find things to fiddle with or you wriggle about when you should be sitting still and concentrating.

BUT, they're also super-cool for doing tricks with, and in this book you'll find **loads of new skills and challenges** to impress your mates with. You'll find out everything, from the basics of getting to know your spinner to twirling it like a pro. Plus there are some **awesome new ways to play** with them and improve your skills.

SKILLS ☆☆☆☆☆

RATE YOURSELF LOOK OUT FOR THE FIVE-STAR RATINGS NEXT TO EACH SKILL AND COLOUR THEM IN TO RATE HOW GOOD YOU ARE AT EACH ONE.

PICK A SPINNER

Fidget Spinners are all pretty small but they come in **LOADS of different shapes!** Which ones of these have you got?

8

In this book we're going to be using this kind but you can give these tricks and challenges a go with whatever spinner you've got and **put your own spin** on them!

AWESOME MODS

Fidget Spinners come in all different colours and patterns, but to make your spinner **really stand out from the crowd**, you could give it some **cool mods**. Here are a few ideas on how to make yours really unique:

USE MARKER PENS TO DRAW ON **GEOMETRIC SHAPES** OR **FUNKY SWIRLS**

GLUE COLOURED PAPER OVER THE BEARINGS TO COVER THE HOLES WITH PATTERNS TOO

Add stickers of your favourite characters, sports teams or bands

Try a **glow in the dark pen** to see your spinner come to life at night!

THINK ABOUT WHAT YOUR DESIGN WILL LOOK LIKE WHEN IT SPINS. YOU COULD EVEN SPIN THE SPINNER AND HOLD YOUR MARKER ON IT WHILE IT SPINS, TO GET A DESIGN THAT GOES THE WHOLE WAY ROUND

TRY ADDING MAGNETS TO THE BEARINGS – HOW DOES IT AFFECT THE SPIN?

ASK IF YOU CAN BORROW SOME NAIL POLISH. PLACE NEWSPAPER UNDERNEATH, SPIN YOUR SPINNER AND FLICK THE BRUSH TO CREATE A **COOL SPLATTER EFFECT**

11

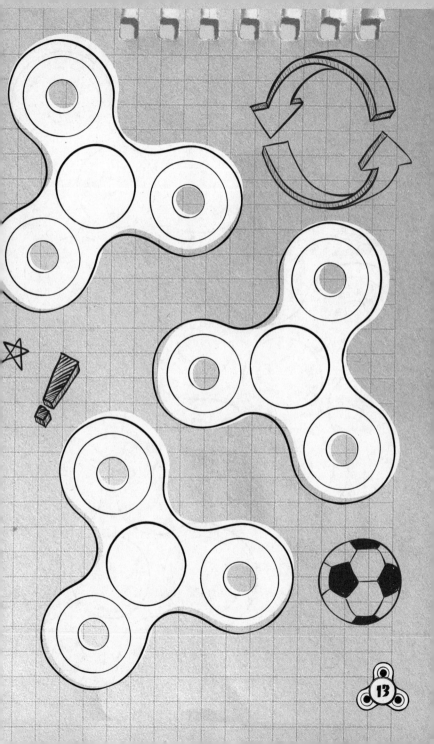

DREAM SPINNER

Now you've thought about all the spinners out there, use these pages to design your **very own ultimate spinner.** What shape is it? How many arms does it have? What makes it different? What would you call it?

THE BASICS

Getting to know your spinner is **key to becoming a pro.** Start off by practising a few simple things and recording your results so you know **what works and what doesn't.**

The Hold Are you left- or right-handed? When you spin it between your thumb and finger, **which finger is the most comfortable** for you? Most people go for the index finger, but maybe the middle finger works better for you. Get used to doing a simple spin and take it from there . . .

I LIKE TO HOLD MY SPINNER

....

Surfaces Some tricks need you to spin it on a flat surface. Where works best? The floor? A table? Outside? Try a few and see how it affects the spin.

MY SPINNER SPINS BEST ON

....

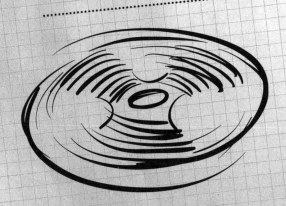

HOW LONG CAN YOU SPIN FOR?

Once you've settled on your favourite ways to spin, **how long can you spin for?** Use this chart to keep track.

	1	2	3	4	5	6	7	8	9	10
HOLDING SPIN										
SURFACE SPIN										

SPIN CYCLE

HOW YOU SPIN IT IS JUST AS IMPORTANT AS HOW LONG YOU CAN SPIN IT FOR! HOW DO YOU SPIN YOURS?

 1 ☆☆☆☆☆

THE TWO HANDER - hold it with one hand and use the other to get it in a spin.

 2 ☆☆☆☆☆

THE FLICK - hold it in one hand and get it spinning with the flick of a wrist.

 3 ☆☆☆☆☆

TAP AND TWIRL - hold it in one hand and tap with a finger on the same hand to make it spin. Try putting your middle finger between two of the arms of the spinner to flick it.

BALANCING

ACT

ONCE YOU CAN KEEP A DECENT SPIN GOING
BETWEEN YOUR THUMB AND A FINGER, IT'S
TIME TO **GRADUATE TO BALANCES.**

The most basic of these is getting it to
balance on the **end of your thumb.** Start
by spinning it with it pinched between
thumb and index finger with your thumb
at the bottom, then gently **lift your
finger away.** ☆☆☆☆☆

Once you've mastered that, **try it on your
index finger** starting with a pinch hold but
with your finger at the bottom and your
thumb on the top. ☆☆☆☆☆

Practise spinning it on each
finger until you can do them
all comfortably. ☆☆☆☆☆

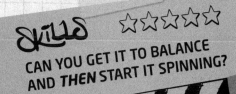

SKILLS ☆☆☆☆☆

CAN YOU GET IT TO BALANCE
AND **THEN** START IT SPINNING?

21

HANDY GUIDE

Use these handy (groan) diagrams to mark up **where you're able to balance your spinner.** Can you do fingertips? Knuckles? The palm of your hands? What about the very tip of your fingers? That's gonna take some practice!

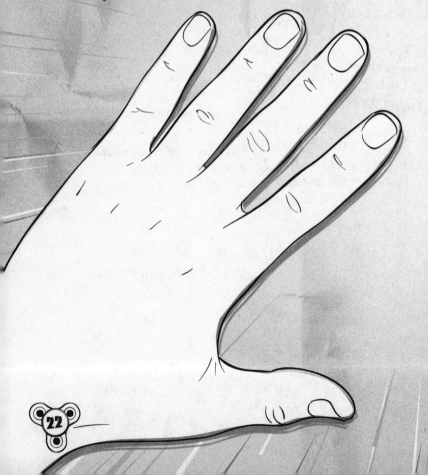

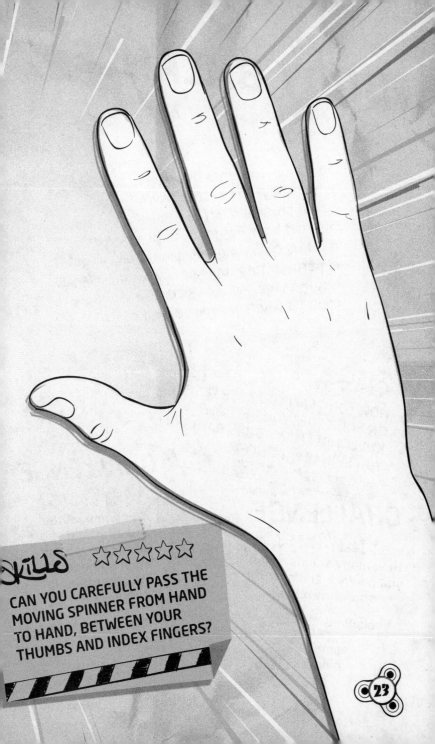

SKILLS ☆☆☆☆☆

CAN YOU CAREFULLY PASS THE MOVING SPINNER FROM HAND TO HAND, BETWEEN YOUR THUMBS AND INDEX FINGERS?

23

BODY BALANCE

So you've mastered the finger spins, but **what about the rest of you?** It's time to get physical and see what else you can do. Your body has loads of points you could try balancing the spinner on, so **get experimenting** and see how many bits you can manage. Put a cross on the diagram opposite wherever you've cracked it.

SKILLS
☆☆☆☆☆

HOW LONG CAN YOU KEEP IT SPINNING ON YOUR TOE? YOUR ELBOW? YOUR KNEE? HOW MANY BODY PARTS CAN YOU SPIN ON AT ONCE?

CHALLENGE
☆☆☆☆☆

How many spinners can you balance and spin **on someone else?**

I balanced ....

spinning spinners on

....

CHALLENGE
☆☆☆☆☆

Get some mates together and see who can spin the most spinners **on themselves** in one go!

The winner was

....

with

.... spinners!

24

FACE IT

There's a fairly major bit of yourself we've not even tried to spin on yet - your face! Now you're gonna want to **be careful with this one.** Rounded edged spinners **only** now please and **tie that long hair back.** We don't want to be responsible for you having to cut a chunk of your hair off because a spinner got stuck in it. Your mum's not going to like that.

Chins are also pretty easy, unless you've got a beard, which is going to make things trickier!

☆☆☆☆☆

Try your forehead first. If you tip your head back, you'll find it's a **pretty simple surface** to balance the spinner on and get it twirling. ☆☆☆☆☆

Finally, give your nose a go. This one needs some **awesome balance**. Watch out for your eyes! ☆☆☆☆☆

CHALLENGE
☆☆☆☆☆

Know any baldies? Give it a spin on the top of their head!
Bonus points if they can stand up and keep it spinning!

27

In a Spin

Test your spins with these **personal and competitive challenges!** You're going to need as many spinners as you can get your hands on for these.

CHALLENGE
☆☆☆☆☆

Place all your spinners on a flat surface and get them all spinning one after another as quickly as you can. How many can you get spinning at once?

CHALLENGE
☆☆☆☆☆

Invite your friends round with all their spinners too. How many can you all get spinning in one go?

CHALLENGE
☆☆☆☆☆

Can you predict which of your spinners will spin the longest? Get them all going at once and see if you guessed right.

CHALLENGE
☆☆☆☆☆

Try the same challenge against your mates. Who can keep a spin going the longest? And who guessed right?

SPIN MASTER

I GOT .... FIDGET SPINNERS
SPINNING IN ONE GO!
DATE .... TIME ....

WE GOT .... FIDGET SPINNERS
SPINNING IN ONE GO!
DATE .... TIME ....

I PREDICTED MY .... WOULD SPIN
THE LONGEST. I WAS RIGHT/WRONG!
IT WAS ....
DATE .... TIME ....

I SPUN AGAINST ....
OUR PREDICTIONS WERE ....
.... WAS RIGHT!
DATE .... TIME ....

So Many Spinners

Take a break from all that spinning and see if you can count how many spinners are on these pages. Why not use your spinner as a timer? Give it a spin and see if you can finish counting before it stops spinning!

(The answer is at the bottom of the page.)

There are 37 spinners on this page, 39 if you count the page numbers.

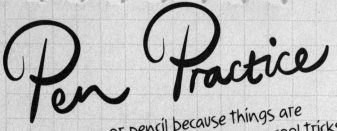

Pen Practice

Grab a pen or pencil because things are about to get sharp! Here are some cool tricks you can do with a pen and a flat surface . . .

SKILLS ☆☆☆☆☆

FIRST UP, TRY SPINNING YOUR SPINNER ON THE **END OF A PEN.** CAN YOU DO IT ON THE FLAT END? HOW ABOUT THE POINT? CRACKED THAT? NOW TRY **LIFTING IT UP IN THE AIR** WHILE IT IS STILL SPINNING. HOW HIGH CAN YOU GO?

SKILLS ☆☆☆☆☆

NOW YOU CAN SPIN IT ON THE END OF A PEN, CAN YOU MAKE IT **JUMP OFF THE END** OF THE PEN AND **CATCH IT AGAIN** WHILE IT'S STILL SPINNING? TRICKY.

REMOVE THE PLASTIC CAPS FROM THE CENTRE BEARING AND TRY PUSHING THE **PEN THROUGH THE MIDDLE** OF THE SPINNER. NOW YOU CAN SPIN THE PEN ON A TABLE. **STAND THE PEN UPRIGHT** AND SPIN THE SPINNER AROUND IT. GIVE IT A FLICK AND THE PEN AND SPINNER WILL MOVE ACROSS THE TABLE TOO. NOW TRY STARTING IT **SPINNING AT AN ANGLE** AND SEE WHAT HAPPENS. (AFTER A FEW SPINS ON ITS SIDE, IT SHOULD STRAIGHTEN UP!)

SPIN ON

WHAT ELSE CAN YOU SPIN YOUR SPINNER ON? GIVE THESE A TRY . . .

Please your parents and **look like you're helping with the housework** by spinning it on the end of a broom or mop!

CHALLENGE
☆☆☆☆☆

What's the smallest thing you can spin on? A coin? A bottle top? Your little brother? How long can you keep it going for?

CHALLENGE
☆☆☆☆☆

Can you spin it on someone **while they're asleep?** Bonus points if you can get it on your dad's nose **without waking him up!**

CHALLENGE
☆☆☆☆☆

Can you spin it on the seat of your bike? Or the handlebars of your scooter? Can you keep it spinning while you ride?

34

Spun On	Success?	Star Ratings

Where's the weirdest or most impressive place you've managed to get a spin going? Keep a record here.

Finger Skills

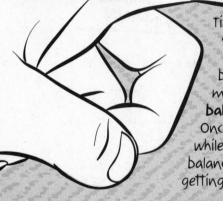

Time for some more handy skills! Let's get back to spinning on your fingers. To be able to do some of the more advanced spinner tricks, **balance is super important.** Once you can **move around** while you've got a spinning balance going, you can start getting **really impressive.**

Skills ☆☆☆☆☆

PRACTISE **LIFTING THE SPINNING SPINNER** WHILE IT'S BALANCED ON THE END OF YOUR FINGER. START WITH YOUR HAND FLAT ON YOUR LAP OR A TABLE AND HOLD THIS BOOK NEXT TO IT. USE THE RULER TO MEASURE HOW FAR YOU'RE ABLE TO GO EACH TIME. ONCE YOU CAN CLEAR THE TOP OF THE BOOK, SEE **HOW MUCH FURTHER YOU CAN REACH!**

CHALLENGE ☆☆☆☆☆

Take on a friend and see who can lift their spinning spinner the highest!

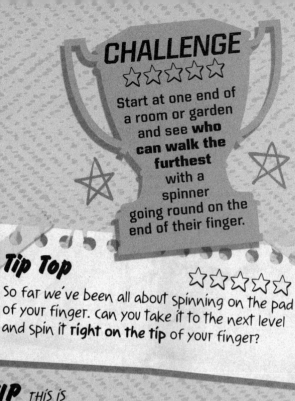

CHALLENGE
☆☆☆☆☆

Start at one end of a room or garden and see **who can walk the furthest** with a spinner going round on the end of their finger.

Tip Top
☆☆☆☆☆

So far we've been all about spinning on the pad of your finger. Can you take it to the next level and spin it **right on the tip** of your finger?

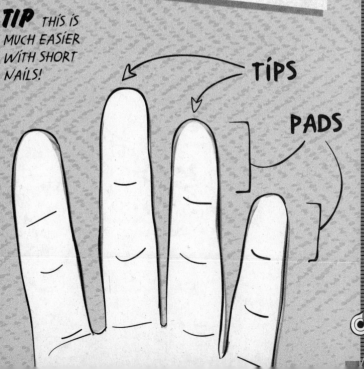

TIP THIS IS MUCH EASIER WITH SHORT NAILS!

TIPS

PADS

SIMPLE FLIP ☆☆☆☆☆

- SPIN THE SPINNER ON THE END OF YOUR FINGER OR THUMB.

- PLACE A FINGER OF THE OPPOSITE HAND ON THE TOP CENTRE OF THE MOVING SPINNER.

- ROTATE YOUR HANDS SO THE HAND UNDERNEATH BECOMES THE HAND ON TOP.

- THE FINGER OR THUMB YOU STARTED ON SHOULD NOW BE ON THE TOP OF THE SPINNER.

- TAKE THAT FINGER OR THUMB AWAY. YOU'VE MOVED THE SPINNER FROM ONE HAND TO THE OTHER!

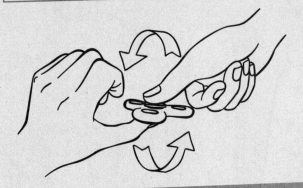

SIMPLE THROW AND CATCH ☆☆☆☆☆

- HOLD THE SPINNER UPRIGHT BETWEEN YOUR THUMB AND INDEX FINGER.
- GIVE IT A SPIN.
- FLICK YOUR WRIST GENTLY UPWARDS AND LET GO OF THE SPINNER.
- CATCH THE SPINNER WITH YOUR THUMB AND INDEX FINGER ON THE CENTRE OF THE SPINNER.
- DID YOU CATCH IT? IS IT STILL SPINNING? AMAZING!

FINGERTIP TRANSFERS ☆☆☆☆☆

KEEPING THE SPINNER IN ONE HAND, CAN YOU MOVE IT FROM FINGER TO FINGER? YOU'RE GOING TO NEED A STEADY HAND FOR THIS ONE!

START WITH THE SPINNER SPINNING ON YOUR INDEX FINGER.

CAREFULLY MOVE YOUR MIDDLE FINGER ACROSS SO THAT BOTH FINGERS ARE UNDER THE CENTRE OF THE SPINNER.

MOVE YOUR INDEX FINGER AWAY SO THAT THE SPINNER IS NOW SPINNING ON YOUR MIDDLE FINGER.

NOW PLACE YOUR RING FINGER UNDER THE CENTRE OF THE SPINNER WITH YOUR MIDDLE FINGER, THEN MOVE THE MIDDLE FINGER AWAY.

FINALLY, PLACE YOUR LITTLE FINGER UNDER THE CENTRE OF THE SPINNER WITH YOUR RING FINGER, THEN MOVE THE RING FINGER AWAY.

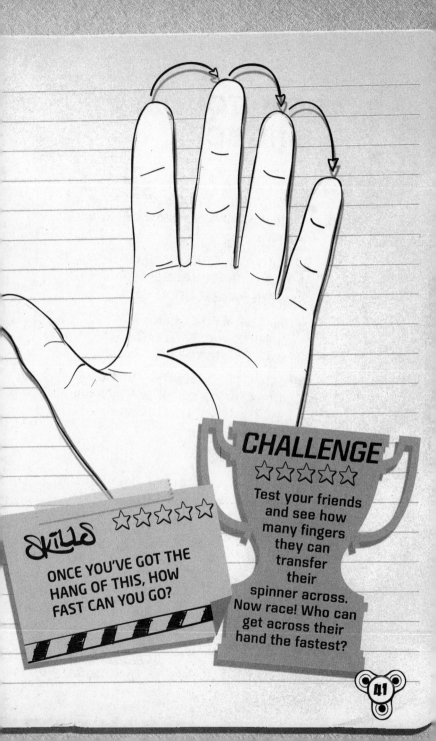

HAND-TO-HAND HOP

☆☆☆☆☆

- SPIN THE SPINNER BETWEEN YOUR THUMB AND INDEX FINGER IN ONE HAND.

- HOLD YOUR OTHER HAND CLOSE TO THIS ONE WITH YOUR FINGERS AND THUMB IN THE SAME POSITION.

- DIP YOUR SPINNER HAND DOWN SLIGHTLY AND GENTLY TOSS THE SPINNER INTO THE AIR.

- CATCH IT BETWEEN THE THUMB AND INDEX FINGER OF THE WAITING HAND.

CHALLENGE

☆☆☆☆☆

Get in a line with your friends and see how far along the row you can pass the moving spinner without dropping it before it stops spinning!

SKILLS ☆☆☆☆☆

CAN YOU GO LEFT TO RIGHT AND RIGHT TO LEFT?

TIP BEND YOUR KNEES SLIGHTLY AS YOU DIP AND THROW!

THE JUMPER ☆☆☆☆☆

HOW WIDE APART CAN YOU HOLD YOUR HANDS WHILE CATCHING THE SPINNER? FOLLOW THE INSTRUCTIONS FOR THE HAND-TO-HAND HOP BUT GRADUALLY TAKE YOUR HANDS WIDER AND WIDER. YOU'LL NEED TO FLICK YOUR WRIST HARDER TO HELP THE SPINNER FLY BETWEEN YOUR HANDS.

SKILLS ☆☆☆☆☆

CAN YOU DO THE HOP WITHOUT LOOKING? WHAT ABOUT THE JUMP?

CHALLENGE ☆☆☆☆☆

Who can take their hands the furthest apart and still catch the spinner while it spins?

THROW AND CATCH

☆☆☆☆☆

FIND YOUR PERFECT PARTNER TO THROW AND CATCH WITH AND SEE WHO YOU CAN KEEP IT GOING THE LONGEST WITH. USE THESE STARS TO KEEP A TALLY.

NAME
Dylan

𝍡

NAME

NAME

NAME

NAME ....

NAME ....

NAME ....

NAME ....

NAME ....

NAME ....

NAME ....

45

THE HIGH HOP

☆☆☆☆☆

- 🌀 WHEN YOU'VE MASTERED THE HAND-TO-HAND HOP, GIVE THIS ONE A GO.

- 🌀 SPIN THE SPINNER BETWEEN YOUR THUMB AND INDEX FINGER IN ONE HAND.

- 🌀 BENDING YOUR KNEES SLIGHTLY, TOSS THE SPINNER UP INTO THE AIR AS HIGH AS YOU CAN. (BEST TO TRY THIS ONE OUTSIDE . . .)

- 🌀 CATCH IT IN YOUR OTHER HAND, STILL SPINNING!

CHALLENGE

⭐⭐⭐☆☆

Get your mates round and see who can throw it the highest and catch it. It only counts if it's still spinning on the catch!

THE FLICK ☆☆☆☆☆

- HOLD THE CENTRE OF THE SPINNER BETWEEN YOUR THUMB AND INDEX FINGER.

- NOW TURN YOUR HAND SO THE SPINNER IS VERTICAL INSTEAD OF HORIZONTAL AND GIVE IT A SPIN.

- FLICK YOUR WRIST AND RELEASE THE SPINNER SO IT JUMPS INTO THE AIR.

- CAN YOU CATCH IT AGAIN BETWEEN YOUR THUMB AND INDEX FINGER?

TIP PRACTISE BY FLICKING IT UP AND CATCHING IT IN THE PALM OF YOUR HAND. WHEN YOU CAN DO THAT, THEN TRY BETWEEN YOUR THUMB AND INDEX FINGER.

 SKILLS ☆☆☆☆☆

CAN YOU FLICK IT SO THE SPIN REVERSES BEFORE YOU CATCH IT? GOOD LUCK WITH THAT ONE!

JUMPING JACK

☆☆☆☆☆

- SPIN THE SPINNER ON THE END OF YOUR FINGER AND HOLD IT STEADY.

- USING YOUR OTHER HAND, GIVE THE ARM THAT IS HOLDING THE SPINNER A BUMP, SO THE SPINNER JUMPS INTO THE AIR.

- CAN YOU CATCH THE SPINNER, STILL SPINNING, ON THE SAME FINGER IT JUMPED OFF?

CHALLENGE

☆☆☆☆☆

Can you jump it off your finger and on to your mate's finger? This needs some serious coordination!

SKILLS ☆☆☆☆☆

HOW HIGH CAN YOU BOUNCE THE SPINNER OFF YOUR FINGER AND STILL CATCH IT? HOW ABOUT CATCHING IT ON A DIFFERENT FINGER?

48

KNUCKLE SPINNER

☆☆☆☆☆

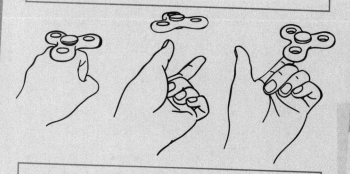

- 🌀 SPIN THE SPINNER ON YOUR KNUCKLE.
- 🌀 FLICK YOUR HAND SO THE SPINNER BOUNCES INTO THE AIR.
- 🌀 WHILE IT'S IN THE AIR, FLIP YOUR HAND OVER AND CATCH IT ON THE END OF YOUR FINGER.

SKILLS ☆☆☆☆☆

CAN YOU CATCH IT ON YOUR FINGER, THEN FLIP IT UP AGAIN AND CATCH IT BACK ON YOUR KNUCKLE? THAT'S SUPER PRO!

GO DARK

Got a glow-in-the-dark or light-up spinner? **Lucky you!** Now go back and practise all the tricks you've already learnt until you can **do them with the lights off!**

REVERSE POLARITY ☆☆☆☆☆

- SPIN THE SPINNER BETWEEN YOUR THUMB AND INDEX FINGER WITH YOUR FINGER AT THE BOTTOM AND YOUR THUMB ON THE TOP.

- RELEASE THE SPINNER AND FLICK IT SLIGHTLY UP INTO THE AIR.

- AT THE SAME TIME, MOVE YOUR HAND SLIGHTLY BACK AND FLIP YOUR HAND OVER.

- GRAB THE SPINNER BETWEEN YOUR THUMB AND INDEX FINGER, THIS TIME WITH YOUR THUMB AT THE BOTTOM AND YOUR FINGER ON THE TOP!

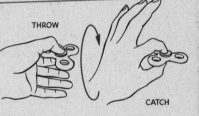

THROW

CATCH

SKILLS ☆☆☆☆☆

HOW MANY TIMES IN A ROW CAN YOU REVERSE THE POLARITY?

CHALLENGE
☆☆☆☆☆
See who can do this the most times in a row – you or a friend?

BACK AND BEYOND ☆☆☆☆☆

- SPIN THE SPINNER BETWEEN YOUR THUMB AND INDEX FINGER.
- PASS YOUR HAND BEHIND YOUR BACK AND GENTLY THROW THE SPINNER TO YOUR OTHER HAND.
- CATCH IT BEHIND YOUR BACK, STILL SPINNING!

TIP WHEN YOU THROW THE SPINNER BEHIND YOUR BACK, TRY THROWING IT IN A CURVE AROUND YOUR WAIST OR FLIPPING IT OVER YOUR SHOULDER SO YOU'RE ACTUALLY CATCHING IT IN FRONT OF YOU!

CHALLENGE
☆☆☆☆☆

How many times can you get the spinner to circle your body before it stops spinning or you drop it?

LEG UP ☆☆☆☆☆

- SPIN THE SPINNER ON THE END OF YOUR FINGER.

- LIFT THE LEG ON THE SAME SIDE OF YOUR BODY AS THE HAND YOU ARE SPINNING ON.

- MOVE YOUR HAND BELOW THE RAISED LEG AND THROW THE SPINNER UNDERNEATH IT.

- CATCH THE SPINNER ON THE FINGER OF YOUR OPPOSITE HAND.

TIP PRACTISE JUST PASSING THE MOVING SPINNER UNDER YOUR LEG BEFORE YOU TRY CATCHING IT. THEN TRY THROWING AND CATCHING BETWEEN YOUR THUMBS AND INDEX FINGERS.

SKILLS ☆☆☆☆☆

CAN YOU CATCH THE SPINNER WITH THE SAME HAND YOU'VE JUST RELEASED IT FROM? YOU'LL NEED TO MOVE QUICKLY!

UNDERARM ☆☆☆☆☆

- SPIN THE SPINNER VERTICALLY BETWEEN YOUR THUMB AND INDEX FINGER.
- THROW THE MOVING SPINNER UNDER THE OPPOSITE ARM.
- CATCH IT WITH THE THUMB AND INDEX FINGER OF YOUR OPPOSITE HAND.

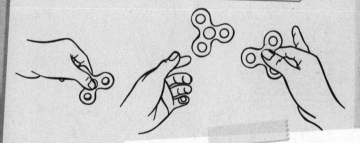

SKILLS ☆☆☆☆☆

WHAT ELSE CAN YOU THROW YOUR SPINNER OVER, UNDER OR THROUGH AND STILL CATCH IT? HOW ABOUT A HULA HOOP?

ORBITAL TILT AND WHIRL ☆☆☆☆☆

- SPIN THE SPINNER ON THE END OF YOUR FINGER.

- TWIST YOUR HAND AROUND SO IT GOES UNDER YOUR ARM WITHOUT DROPPING THE SPINNER.

- CAN YOU LIFT YOUR HAND UP IN THE AIR AND KEEP IT SWIRLING AROUND YOUR BODY WITH THE SPINNER STILL GOING?

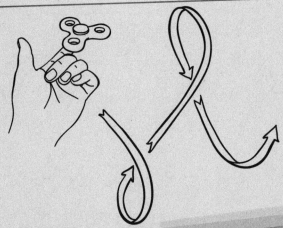

SKILLS ☆☆☆☆☆

THE BIGGER THE ARM MOVEMENTS, THE GREATER THE SKILLS! HOW MUCH CAN YOU TILT AND WHIRL BEFORE YOU DROP IT?

THE JUGGLER ☆☆☆☆☆

- YOU'RE GOING TO NEED TWO SPINNERS FOR THIS ONE!

- GET A SPINNER SPINNING IN EACH HAND, BETWEEN YOUR THUMBS AND INDEX FINGERS.

- SLIGHTLY RAISE ONE HAND AND LOWER THE OTHER.

- AT THE SAME TIME, THROW THE SPINNERS TOWARDS THE OPPOSITE HANDS.

- CATCH THE SPINNERS BETWEEN YOUR THUMBS AND INDEX FINGERS.

TIP MAKE SURE YOU'VE REALLY MASTERED CATCHING LEFT TO RIGHT AND RIGHT TO LEFT BEFORE YOU START WORKING ON THIS ONE!

SKILLS ☆☆☆☆☆

CAN YOU JUGGLE MORE THAN TWO? INSANE SKILLS!

SOCCER SPINNING

IF YOU'VE GOT BALL SKILLS, TRY DOING SOME OF THE SAME TRICKS WITH YOUR FIDGET SPINNER!

KEEPY UPPIES ☆☆☆☆☆

- SPIN THE SPINNER ON THE END OF YOUR FINGER AND HOLD IT STEADY.
- USING YOUR OTHER HAND, GIVE THE ARM THAT IS HOLDING THE SPINNER A BUMP, SO THE SPINNER JUMPS INTO THE AIR.
- CAN YOU CATCH THE SPINNER, STILL SPINNING, ON THE SAME FINGER IT JUMPED OFF?
- BUMP IT UP AGAIN, OVER AND OVER.

SKILLS ☆☆☆☆☆

CAN YOU BOUNCE IT FROM KNEE TO KNEE?

TIP TRY STARTING THIS BY STARTING IT SPINNING ON YOUR KNEE INSTEAD OF DROPPING IT ON TO THE KNEE.

FOOT TRICKS ☆☆☆☆☆

- SPIN THE SPINNER BETWEEN YOUR THUMB AND INDEX FINGER.

- DROP THE SPINNER TOWARDS YOUR FOOT AND LIFT THE OPPOSITE LEG UP AND OVER THE TOP OF IT.

- LAND THE SPINNER ON YOUR FOOT OR KICK IT UP!

KICK AND CATCH ☆☆☆☆☆

- SPIN THE SPINNER ON YOUR FOOT.

- KICK IT UP INTO THE AIR.

- BEND OVER AND CATCH IT ON YOUR BACK OR THE BACK OF YOUR NECK!

STACKS OF FUN

You must be exhausted after all that, but don't worry, **you can sit down for these tricks!** You're going to need as many fidget Spinners as you can get your hands on . . .

Start off by placing one spinner on top of another and getting them both spinning. ☆☆☆☆☆

Now try spinning the two in different directions! ☆☆☆☆☆

Can you spin one *then* place another on top of it? ☆☆☆☆☆

How many can you stack and spin in one go? Colour in the pile opposite to show how high you can go! ☆☆☆☆☆

Bring your friends and their collections together for a mega stack challenge!

Who can build the highest stack?

Whose stack can spin the longest?

Can you stack a mixture of different shaped spinners?

Does every spinner have to be spinning at once?

Can you get alternate spinners spinning?

Which spinner in the stack spins the longest?

RULES AND RESULTS

☆☆☆☆☆

USE THIS PAGE TO RECORD THE RULES
AND RESULTS OF YOUR GAME:

1. ....
....

2. ....
....

3. ....
....

4. ....
....

The winner was ....

They stacked .... spinners.

The best thing about it was ....

....

CHALLENGE CHOOSERS

Trying these challenges or creating your own? Use your spinner to help decide the rules of the game. Put a bit of sticky tape on one arm of your spinner. **Place your spinner on these pages.** Write your names in the spaces in the left-hand circle, then **spin the spinner.** Wherever the arm with the tape on lands, that person takes on the challenge or goes first! Then use the second wheel to choose the challenge!

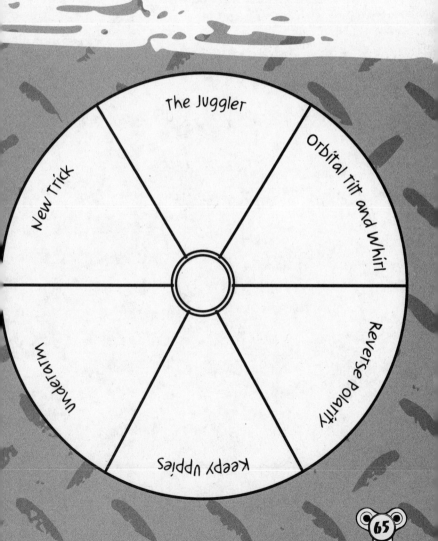

The Juggler

Orbital Tilt and Whirl

New Trick

Reverse Polarity

Underarm

Keepy Uppies

BALANCE BALL

SPIN TO SEE WHERE TO
BALANCE YOUR SPINNER!

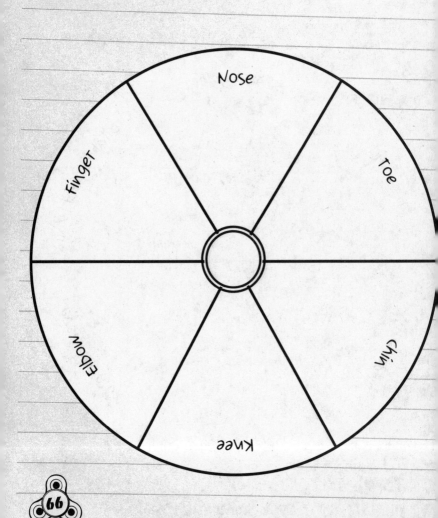

Who Dares Spins

A parent

The branch of a tree

The TV

A piece of fruit

The end of a fork

Your bed

CHALLENGE MAKERS

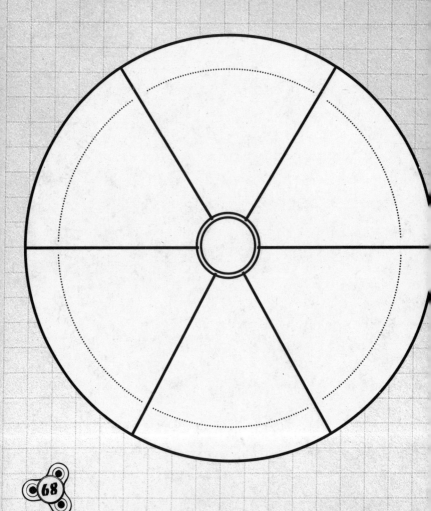

USE THESE SPINNERS TO **CREATE YOUR OWN GAMES AND CHALLENGES** BY WRITING YOUR TRICKS, DARES OR CHALLENGES IN THE SPACES AND GIVING YOUR SPINNER A WHIRL.

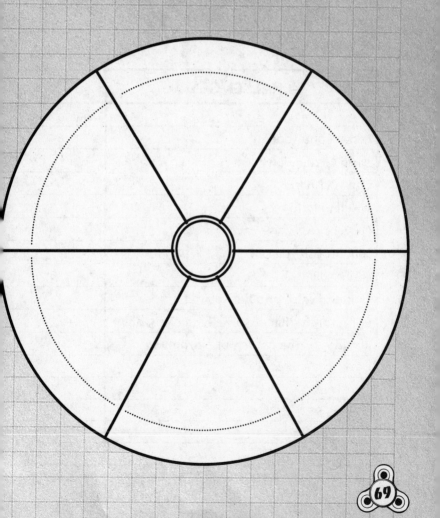

TIME CHALLENGES

See how many times you can do each of these things in the **time it takes your spinner to stop spinning!** Add your own challenges to the end of the list.

CHALLENGES	
	Name: ....
Hop on one foot	
Jump up and down	
Clap your hands	
Jumping jack	
Press up	
Spin around yourself	
Write your name	
Flick and catch another spinner	
Eat a raisin, chip or something else small	
Run laps of the garden or playground	

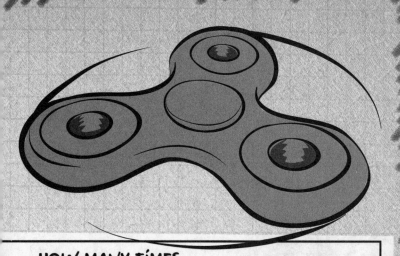

HOW MANY TIMES

Name:	Name:	Name: ....

BALANCE ME

With your spinner on a flat surface, you can **balance all kinds of things** on it as it spins! Try carefully lowering a glass of water on to the top of it as it goes round without spilling a drop!

RATE HOW EASY OR HARD YOU FOUND IT TO BALANCE THESE THINGS ON YOUR SPINNER:

ANOTHER SPINNER
☆☆☆☆☆

A DRINK
☆☆☆☆☆

A mini figure
☆☆☆☆☆

A small ball
☆☆☆☆☆

A MOBILE PHONE
☆☆☆☆☆

A KEY
☆☆☆☆☆

A COIN
☆☆☆☆☆

AN APPLE
☆☆☆☆☆

CHALLENGE
☆☆☆☆☆

What's the strangest thing you can balance on your spinner?

CHALLENGE
☆☆☆☆☆

Who can balance the most different things on one moving spinner before it stops spinning?

CHALLENGE
☆☆☆☆☆

Who can build the highest pile of coins on a moving spinner before they fall?

CHALLENGE
☆☆☆☆☆

What else have you managed to balance?

OUTDOOR FUN

it's not all about spinning, you know. Why not try mixing up some traditional outdoor games and activities by adding your own spin to them? Here are a few to get you started . . .

SKITTLES ☆☆☆☆☆

You'll need some **flat ground** (not grass) and some **empty plastic bottles** for this one. Set the bottles up as shown in the picture then walk back a short distance. Each player takes turns **skimming and sliding** their spinner across the ground to see **how many bottles they can knock down.** Score one point for each bottle you knock down, but double if it you get all six down in one go. **Strike!**

PLAYER	SCORES									
	1	2	3	4	5	6	7	8	9	10

ZIP-WIRE RACES ☆☆☆☆☆

Get a piece of string for each player and **tie one end to a fence** or something high up. Thread the other end of each string through a fidget spinner, then tie the ends to a broom handle or something that will keep them flat and stretched out at an angle forming a slope. Each player pulls their fidget spinner to the top of the string and let's go! **Whose will reach the ground first?**

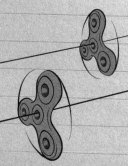

Use this space to **make up your own game.** Can you think of a game you can add your own spinner twist to? Or make up something completely new! **What are the rules** and **how do you win?**

75

THE SPIN GAMES

It's time for an **epic spinner challenge:** the Spin Games. For this, you'll need some **worthy competitors,** each ready to try and prove themselves across a number of Fidget Spinner sports. You could even get into teams and **put your best player forward** in each challenge. Good luck, and **may the best spinner win!**

Score 10 points for first place, 5 points for second and 2 points for third. Dropping the spinner means you're disqualified from that round!

SPEED RACER ☆☆☆☆☆

Pick two points in your garden or the park to race between. Each competitor gets the spinner spinning on their finger and then it's **ready, steady, GO!**

FIRST ....

SECOND ....

THIRD ....

LONG DISTANCE ★☆☆☆☆

This one is all about how far you can go with the spinner still balancing and spinning. You can walk or run and the one who **keeps moving the longest** wins!

FIRST ....

SECOND ....

THIRD ....

HIGH JUMP ★☆☆☆☆

Spin the spinner between your thumb and index finger then toss it up into the air and catch it. The person who can throw it the highest and still catch it wins.

FIRST ....

SECOND ....

THIRD ....

LONG JUMP ★☆☆☆☆

Spin your spinner between your thumb and index finger then toss it to your other hand. Catch the spinner while it's still spinning. The further you can open your arms and still catch it, the more points you get!

FIRST ....

SECOND ....

THIRD ....

TENNIS ☆☆☆☆☆

Play this one in pairs, standing opposite one another. The object of the game is to throw and catch the spinner with the other player for as long as possible.

SCORING

If you can throw and catch twice each in a row, score two points each, then an extra point for each additional catch.

If you throw the spinner wildly and it means the other player has no chance of catching it, lose two points.

Use this space to keep a note of the scores:

PLAYER ONE ....

PLAYER TWO ....

PLAYER THREE ....

PLAYER FOUR ....

HOCKEY ☆☆☆☆☆

For this one you need a table, one spinner and two players.

Position a player at each end of the table. The youngest player starts with the spinner.

Place the spinner on the table and spin it. Knock the spinner across the table towards the other player.

If the spinner flies off the end of the table, GOAL! You score a point.

If the player opposite catches it or manages to knock it back, or if it goes off the side of the table, no score!

Give yourselves ten minutes and see who can score the most points.

PLAYER ONE ....

PLAYER TWO ....

PLAYER THREE ....

PLAYER FOUR ....

CURLING ☆☆☆☆☆

You'll need a broom to play this one, and each player will need a Fidget Spinner of a different colour. You'll also need a flat playing surface, like a wooden or tiled floor and some masking tape.

Use the **masking tape to mark an X** on the floor as a target.

Starting at the opposite end of the room, spin your spinner on the floor then **use the broom to nudge it** towards the target. The spinner should spin and slide across the floor.

The next player then starts from the same place and nudges their spinner across the floor.

The aim of the game is to **get your spinner closest to the target X.**

FIRST ....

SECOND ....

THIRD ....

TIP IT'S OK TO KNOCK YOUR OPPONENT'S SPINNER OUT OF THE WAY WITH YOUR OWN!

80

MORE SPORTS

There are so many different sports. Why not pick some others to put your own spin on?

How about **gymnastics?** Can you roll, backflip and twirl yourself while keeping the spinner moving?

Make a raised slope with a piece of wood or cardboard and try **ski jumping!** How far off the end of your jump will the spinner fly?

Pair up with a mate and get your **synchronized spinning** on! Can you do the same tricks at the same time? Double awesome!

AND THE WINNER IS ...

Get a piece of string or ribbon and tie it through one hole of the spinner to **make a medal!** Award the Ultimate Fidget Spinner Games Medal to whoever scored the most points across all the challenges!

ULTIMATE
FIDGET
SPINNER

NEW TRICKS

Use these pages to **note down your own tricks.** Maybe you could create a combo of the things you've learnt here - the more moves you can put together, the **more awesome your skills!** Or try mixing it up by adding spins of your own, or doing the **tricks on a trampoline!** Whatever makes your trick look **unique!**

A CLASS ACT

NOW, YOU MAY HAVE NOTICED THAT A LOT OF TEACHERS AND PARENTS **DON'T LOVE YOUR SPINNER** AS MUCH AS YOU DO. IN FACT, LOTS OF SCHOOLS HAVE ALREADY BANNED THEM. **ARE THEY MAD?** HERE'S HOW TO CONVINCE THEM TO LET YOU **USE YOUR FIDGET SPINNER IN CLASS . . .**

ENGLISH

The spinner is a **useful storytelling tool, honest.**
Use your spinners and your imagination to make up a story. Grab a few spinners and stick a random word on the arm of each one. Set them all spinning and use your finger to stop them by pressing on the arms. **Take the words** on those arms and **make up a story** using them. Here are some words to get you started:

NOUNS

Bacon	Football	Fidget Spinner	Fish
Superhero	Tree	Pirate	Rocket
Camera	Balloon	Footprint	
Banana	Book	Ghost	

ADJECTIVES

Scary	Green	Wobbly
Hot	Wet	Smelly
Mysterious	Sparkly	Grumpy
	Spooky	

Write your story here:

ART

Stick a pencil or felt-tip pen through one of the holes on your spinner and place it on a sheet of paper. Give it a twirl and **see what patterns you can make.** Use these pages to practise.

MATH

Math teachers love shapes and they're also **big fans of averages.** Convince them your spinner is perfect for some **number-based fun** with this simple experiment. You'll need a timer and you can record your results below.

- Each person takes their spinner and takes turns spinning it flat on the table.

- Use the timer to see how long each one spins for.

- Once everyone has had a turn at spinning their spinner, add up all the times.

- Divide the number you have by the number of people who spun a spinner.

- This number is the average spin time of all the spinners!

$$\text{average} = \frac{\text{total times}}{\text{number of spinners}}$$

RESULTS

SPINNER	SHAPE	TIME

The total time of all the spinners is ....

The average time the spinners spun for is ....

Try the experiment again with lots of **different shaped spinners.** Can you work out the average spin time for each shape? Which shape can spin the longest?

What Next?

So you're still not allowed to take your fidget spinner to school and your mum is **threatening to chuck it out** if she sees it one more time. What else could you use it for?

A CEILING FAN FOR YOUR HAMSTER'S CAGE

A PROPELLER FOR A TINY PLANE

A bird feeder

A FASHION ACCESSORY

A PENCIL STORAGE RACK

SPINVENTIONS

What else could you use it for?
Draw your own ideas here.

TROPHY CABINET

There are over 80 tricks and challenges in this book. Colour in the trophies below when you can do each of these, then turn the page to **award yourself the biggest trophy of all** when you've completed them all!

SIMPLE FLIP

PASS BETWEEN HANDS

SPIN WITH ONE HAND

UNDERARM

SPIN ON FINGER

FINGERTIP TRANSFER

SIMPLE THROW AND CATCH

HAND-TO-HAND HOP

SPIN ON FACE

SPIN ON PEN

THE HIGH HOP

JUMPING JACK

LEG UP

THE JUMPER

THE FLICK

CATCH ON PEN

KNUCKLE SPINNER

ORBITAL TILT AND WHIRL

FOOT TRICKS

REVERSE POLARITY

KEEPIE UPPIES

BACK AND BEYOND

THE JUGGLER

KICK AND CATCH

ULTIMATE SPIN MASTER CHAMPION

This trophy for the
ULTIMATE SPIN MASTER CHAMPION
was awarded to

....

On ....

Their specialist skill is

....